My Special Day in Jasper, TX USA

In Memory Of Martha

Jermaine Kenyatta

To order additional copies of this book, contact:
Xlibris Corporation
1-888-795-4274
www.Xlibris.com
Orders@Xlibris.com

Introduction

I think about the hundreds, perhaps thousands of black children across the country during the turbulent 1950's and 1960's that were in the same situation I found myself in. That situation was being the first child to integrate a school or a school system. Many of us did not receive the spectacular publicity of Linda Brown in Topeka, Kansas or Ruby Bridges in New Orleans, Louisiana. Brown's situation came as a result of the landmark court case Brown vs. Board of Education of Topeka, Kansas, that struck down so called separate but equal school policies. Ruby Bridges was the first black child to integrate the New Orleans school district, a large metropolitan area where she was met with a lot of resistance.

These ladies are two people I have admired down though the years because of their courage. I feel a kindred spirit with them. I want to say to all of the others who went through the same situation in big town or small town America, thank you for your efforts and your sacrifices. I want you to know that you all did something that was very important. I feel blessed and privileged to be able to say with all humbleness of mind, that I was one of the first. Thank God that I was counted worthy to be used to pave the way for others.

Written by the late Martha Adams, Summer, 2000

MY SPECIAL DAY
IN JASPER TEXAS USA
IN MEMORY OF MARTHA
WHY ME?

"Momma, why do I have to go?" I asked.

"Because I said so, girl. It's because it's your right to go. Folks have died for you to have this privilege."

I didn't know what Momma meant at the time, but I later understood when I got older. Momma was talking about the black and white people who had gotten killed during the Civil Rights Movement. These people had tried to make life in America better for black folks.

"Baby, you are making history," Momma said. "You are putting an end to segregation in this town, in the elementary school."

"Momma, what is segre – segregation?" I asked. I could hardly say the word. Momma said it means separating the races. Separating colored folk and white folk. Separating public restrooms. Separating eating places in public. Separating schools. Separating everything.

Sometimes, Momma would say colored and sometimes she would say black. Momma said we are going to start saying black instead of colored because these days using the word black gave people of color more pride in their heritage and culture. But sometimes Momma was so used to saying the word, she would forget and say colored and I would too.

"This is 1968 and it's a new day now."

"Some folks say separate is O.K., as long as it's equal. The problem is, it's not equal, child. At the all colored school, you are sent the bent up, broken down desks and the raggedy books, while all the new stuff goes to the all white school. Well, this year you're going to have all the best equipment, desks, books and everything, because you are going to the white school."

"But Momma, none of the other colored kids are going. Why do I have to go?"

"I told you about questioning me," Momma yelled. Then Momma changed her tone. She thought a long time while really looking away. She was just staring at nothing at all. She finally said, in a soft voice, her lips barely moving, "Baby, Momma wants what is best for you."

"You have to be brave. You have to be strong. Baby, you are the first colored child to attend a white elementary school in Jasper, Texas. You are somebody special!"

That made me feel so good, that Momma told me I was somebody special.

"Baby, you are doing this not just for Momma, not just for yourself, but for your whole race."

"But, Momma, why aren't any of the other girls in the family going besides me?"

Momma thought again. She said, "You remember the family reunion we went to and the older girls and boys went to the swimming hole? The water was kind of cold so nobody really wanted to go in right then. Finally, your cousin, Jake, eased out into the water and started swimming around. One, then two and finally, all of your cousins jumped in and started swimming. Well, Baby, you are going to test the water and before you know it, all the colored children will be right there with you."

"Really, Momma?"

"Yes, Baby," Momma said. I later found out, when I grew older, that Momma was just as scared as I was, but she later told me it was something she felt compelled to do.

MY FIRST DAY AT SCHOOL

When Momma dragged me off to school, she said, "Remember child, if you get called names, don't worry about it. Don't call names back. If you get picked on, you tell the teacher. Do you hear?"

"Yes ma'am," I said. I knew I wasn't going to bother anybody but if I got "hemmed into a corner," I had already made up my mind, I was going to come out swinging like Muhammad Ali.

I could feel the cold stares as I walked down the hall. It said on my information card to go to room 311.

The children stared and pointed. The grown ups stared and whispered. There were white faces all around. All staring. I checked to see if my plaits had come loose or my slip was dragging or something. Finally, I said to myself, they are staring at me because I'm the only colored person here.

I felt surrounded. I felt smothered. I was in a crowd of people, but I was all alone.

Just as I had made up my mind to start running for the front door, I saw a friendly face.

"Hello, I'm your teacher. My name is Mrs. Gannon. You must be Martha."

"Yes ma'am."

"Well, welcome to my class. How old are you?"

"I'm 11 years old," I said

"How old are you?" I asked. Mrs. Gannon blushed and then smiled. "Well, we won't talk about that." I said to myself, "I did it again." Momma said sometimes I talked too much and I asked the wrong questions. I was just so glad to have somebody to talk to; I was just talking. We really got to know each other better later on.

Mrs. Gannon was like a fairy Godmother to me. She had a nice glowing smile. She was always quick to pat me on the back or stroke my hair. She would pinch me on the cheek and tell me what a nice dimple I had.

She was slim. She had auburn hair that flowed to her shoulders. Mrs. Gannon had the round rim glasses that I call "granny glasses." She had blue eyes that seemed to look right through you and make you feel warm at the same time. She never talked loud, but she didn't need to. She had a strong voice. Whenever she opened her mouth, she had everybody's attention. She walked and moved around the room like a swan that was in the water.

WHAT DID YOU SAY ABOUT MY MOMMA?

Martha's Mom

I couldn't wait to get back to the neighborhood and see all my friends. I wondered how they got along at school today. I couldn't wait to see Bobby. I wouldn't dare tell Momma that I had a "crush" on him.

At the colored playground, some of my friends were giving me the cold shoulder. "My momma says you think you're something cause you go to the white school. You think you are better than all the other black kids, now. You think you are really something but my momma says you are nothing but a bunch of Uncle Toms. You and your momma."

"What you say to me, girl?"

It was Big Beulah, running her big mouth.

"You hear me, Uncle Tom?"

"What you say about my momma? I'll bet you won't say that in my face."

The girl was about 10 steps closer, but she was still about 10 feet away.

"Uncle Tom, Uncle Tom!"

"You're still not in my face and still not in my space." She finally made the mistake of getting up in my face, calling my momma an Uncle Tom. I sprang on her like a bobcat. I was on her and she was on the ground in one motion. I did her like Momma did me when I was bad. I whipped her and talked to her at the same time. "What you say about my momma?" My best friend, Cindy, and her sister, Cassie, pulled me off of her. We are both crying because of her. She was crying because of the lick I just put on her head. I was crying because of the words that wounded my heart.

Cindy grabbed me by the hand and said "Come on girl, let's get out of here. Don't pay any attention to her. I think you are going to be alright. My mom says if everything works out for you, she is going to send me to the white school next year."

"I overheard my mom tell my dad that she hopes you don't go over there acting all militant and stuff. You didn't, did you?"

"Acting militant! Girl, I don't even know what that means, do you?"

"No, but it must be awful important."

For supper that evening, Momma had cooked my favorite meal; black-eyed peas, cornbread, chicken and dumplings and sweet potato pie. I didn't have much of an appetite, though.

"Lord, child, you haven't eaten a thing and I cooked your favorite meal. What's the matter? I thought everything went pretty well today. Seems like you have a nice teacher."

I interrupted Momma, "What's a militant?"

"Girl, what do you know about a militant?"

"I don't know nothing about it Momma, that's why I'm asking."

"Where did you hear about this, on TV?"

"No, ma'am, one of my friends said they heard their mom say they hope I don't go to the white school acting all militant."

"Well, a militant is a black person that don't much like white people. A militant will use violence as a way to get what they want from white people. That's the best I can explain it."

"Are we militants, Momma?"

"Lord, no child, you know we have taught you to love everybody. Does that sound like a militant to you?"

"No, ma'am. So, I guess that means we are Uncle Toms."

"Where did you get a notion like that?"

"Beulah said her Momma said that cause I go to the white school, we are all Uncle Toms. Exactly what is an Uncle Tom?"

"Well, they go along with just about anything white folk say and they'll go against their own race for the white man, even when the white man's wrong."

"We be Uncle Toms, Momma?"

"No, child. We are not Uncle Toms." Momma stood with her hands on her hips. Momma mumbled something under her breath about the lady that had called us Uncle Toms.

"So calling somebody an Uncle Tom is an awful powerful insult. Can you explain it a little more? Why would someone want to be an Uncle Tom?"

"Well, Baby, an Uncle Tom is a black person that will do anything a white person tells them to do. They feel like they are less and beneath white people. Like I said, they will even turn against their own black race to please the white man."

"Now, we come from four generations of proud black people. It's a lot of white folks that don't want you to succeed at that school, but we are sending you anyway. So, is that being an Uncle Tom?"

"No, ma'am."

"Baby, you are not a militant and you are not an Uncle Tom. You are just a little black girl that's fulfilling Dr. Martin Luther King's dream."

"What is his dream, Momma?"

"He said that one day, little black children will go to school together and play together and learn together with little white children."

"I guess he hasn't been to the school I went to today."

We both started laughing.

"It's coming, child. The Bible says "cast your bread upon the water and in a few days, it shall return."

"What does that mean?"

"It means that what you are doing will pay off one day. Listen child, Dr. King says that in his dream, a child will not be judged by the color of their skin, but the content of their character. What that means, child is you'll be judged by how you act, not by who you are and what color you are."

"The only thing now, though Momma, is that most of the white kids won't talk to me and now most of the black kids hate me, too, just because I go to the white school."

"I'm trapped in the middle Momma, everybody is against me."

"The black kids don't hate you, child, and the white kids will get used to you."

"What it is, baby, is that some folks, black and white, is just afraid of change. When things go on for so long, some folks just think that's the way things ought to be. Be grateful, baby, the Lord is using you to help make a change. You go to that school and you just be yourself. Don't try to be what the white kids want you to be or what the black kids want you to be. If you will just go and be yourself, that will be good enough. Remember, you aren't alone. You'll always have Jesus and you'll always have me."

A NEW FRIEND

I had some good days and some bad days that year. Some of them I've forgotten, but there were two particularly bad incidents that I will never forget.

I had made a friend of one of the white girls in my class. We played together. We laughed and talked about everything that little fifth grade girls talk about. We laughed as she wondered what she would look like in plaits, and I wondered what I would look like with my hair flowing down my back. We played hop-scotch together. We jumped rope together. Her name was Becky.

A New Friend

On this particular day, as we were leaving the school house to wait for our rides, Becky and I walked together as usual. I remember a big white guy walking up in a policeman's uniform and catching her by the hand. "This is my dad," she said proudly.

"How do you do, sir?" I said.

He didn't even look at me. I walked off thinking maybe he didn't hear me. Well, I found out the next day that he heard me alright and he sure saw me. My friend told me the next day, with tears in her eyes, that her father said she was not to play with me anymore.

"Why?" I said, fighting back tears myself.

"He said I am not to have dealings with colored children."

I never will forget the way she said it. She said it as if I had the plague or as if when she touched me some of my black would rub off and get on her. I remembered how hard I had gotten hit one day, while trying to play tackle football with my brother and some of his buddies. Well, what she said to me, hit me harder.

A Rodeo Day

I never shall forget rodeo day in Jasper. It was supposed to be a special day. All of the kids, including myself, were excited because Mrs. Gannon had told us that a rodeo clown was coming to visit us on this day. When the clown finally came in the door, the excitement peaked. We could hardly contain ourselves. I really felt like I belonged. I really felt like, man, I'm part of this class! We were grinning at the clown and grinning at each other.

I had seen a clown at a parade, but I had never seen one up close before. He was showing us clown tricks and he was drawing rodeo pictures, mostly horses and bulls. He then started drawing a cowgirl on the chalkboard. This was the drawing I liked the best. As he was drawing the cowgirl, he was looking straight at me. This really made me feel special. He was drawing me as the cowgirl. Then, he drew an earring in the cowgirl's ear and I knew he was drawing me because I was the only girl in the room with earrings on. It really made me feel good.

Then he said, "Oh, I messed up my cowgirl by drawing the earring in her ear. A real cowgirl would never wear an earring." My heart dropped. I felt like a balloon that someone had blown up, just so they could stick a pin in it and watch it pop. I wanted to pull my earrings out of my ears and run out of the room. I was so embarrassed. It was one of the most hateful things that anybody has ever done to me. I found out that day that clowns can be clowns in more ways than one.

Martha's Teacher

One day at recess I was minding my own business all by myself as usual. I had gotten up to 100 jumps in a row without a miss while I was jumping rope. Then these three white boys came over to where I was and started making fun of me. They said some pretty awful things to me. I tried to just ignore them like Momma said, until one of them called me ugly. At first I started to get all indignant, but as I looked at these three jokers I couldn't help but laugh. They looked like they had just stepped out of a comic strip or a cartoon on TV. One was a short and stumpy version of Alfalfa on the "Little Rascals." The other had a body like Porky Pig and a face like Elmer Fudd. The third one had a profile that compared to him made Frankenstein look like Prince Charming. What a mug shot!

I couldn't help it. I laughed so hard that I lost my balance and fell down. They probably thought I was crazy. Instead of calling them names and punching them out, I wanted to walk up and thank them. This was one of the best laughs I had had in a long time. It goes back to one of Momma's old sayings, "The Pot sure can't call the Kettle Black." These guys were trying to call me ugly, but they sure fit the description of ugly much better than I did.

I look back on those days and I see that my sense of humor really helped to sustain me through some tough times.

I WAS SO AFRAID THAT I DIDN'T SAY A WORD

I never will forget the day that I tried to sharpen a crayola in the pencil sharpener. It messed the pencil sharpener up, big time! Nobody was really looking when I did it. I was so afraid that I didn't say a word. I went back to my seat like nothing had happened. Just about the time I got back to my seat, Mrs. Gannon saw one of the children trying to use the sharpener, but it wouldn't work.

"Did you put a crayon in that sharpener?" Mrs. Gannon asked the child who was using the sharpener. "No, ma'am", he said.

"Do you know who did?" asked Mrs. Gannon.

"No, ma'am", he said.

"Does anybody know who did this?" Nobody said a word. I wanted to confess, but it froze in my throat. I couldn't get it out. I was too embarrassed. Mrs. Gannon was getting upset.

"Okay", she said. "Everybody put their heads down on their desks and close your eyes. Now, nobody is looking and I want the person who did this to raise your hand, now!!"

I finally put my hand up. It was trembling like a leaf in a breeze. Mrs. Gannon said, "Oh, thank you class". She never called my name. She never said another word about it. I think she knew I didn't mean to damage the pencil sharpener and she didn't expose me to the class. That's when I knew her smiling face was not a put on. This lady was for real. She was really my friend.

THE SPECIAL DAY

This is the day that changed my life forever. I call it my Special Day. A big field trip had been planned for the fifth grade. We were to go to the library downtown on this day. I had been telling my teacher for two or three days that I never got a permission slip to be sent home and signed like the other children in my class. She just smiled and kept putting me off. Today, she called me to the side and told me that the reason I didn't get a permission slip is because I was to be her special helper that day. She had chosen me among all her students to be a special helper. It really made me feel important.

While the other children were bussed off to the library with other adults and teachers as chaperones, I rode with Mrs. Gannon in her car. She had the cleanest 1957 Chevy you ever saw. She said you and I won't be going to the library, we have a busy schedule today. We stopped off at the post office. Then we went to the grocery store.

1957 Chevy

What a special day that was for me. Just me and the teacher riding all around town. There were no mean looks staring at me that day. No finger pointing. No name calling. It was like on this day, hatred took a holiday.

16

We got back in time for school dismissal. All of the children were talking about what a special day they had had at the library. I was thinking to myself, their day could not have been any more special than mine.

Years have passed and I am now a teacher myself. I am an elementary school teacher. I also found out some time later just how special that day was and what a special teacher I had. You see, during that time, blacks were not allowed at the public library. My teacher knew I would be the only student in the class who would not be allowed entry to the library. She never told me you can't go to the library because you're black. She could have told me to stay home that day. She could have made me stay on the bus. Instead, she did something to keep me from feeling the hurt from an experience like that. She turned what could have been a horrible day in my life experience, into a special day for me. I will never forget what she did for me on that day.

Thanks to my mom and thanks to Mrs. Gannon, I survived as the first black fifth grader to attend a previously all white school in Jasper, Texas. The experience did not defeat me or destroy me, but it made me spiritually and mentally, a stronger person.

My town, Jasper, Texas, has had some bad publicity a few years back because of a vicious murder of a black man, Mr. James Byrd, by three white men. I can't speak for the whole town, but as far as I can see, prejudice and racism is still alive and well, but everybody in Jasper can't be judged by the actions of a few. But, you know what, I take a little piece of my mom and a little piece of Mrs. Gannon into the classroom with me every day. If I can instill in all my students, black and white, the principles that my mom and Mrs. Gannon instilled in me, I am very optimistic that there is still hope for improvement in race relations for not only Jasper, but all of America. I love this little town. I've been here all my life, and hopefully I can be one of the ones in life that make a positive difference.

Footnote. This story was written in 2000. In 2005 Martha Adams died after a battle with cancer. In her lifetime she did make a difference.

Epilogue

This story is dedicated to the late Martha "Mackie" Adams. She was not able to survive cancer, but she was able to survive life as it was dealt to her, with courage and dignity.

This story is also dedicated to the people all over the country who were the first to integrate their various schools.

It is also about a town that is still living in the shadow of tragic incident. That incident of course was the murder of Mr. James Byrd a little over 10 years ago. A hate crimes bill was recently passed all over this country to increase punishment for people like the ones who murdered Mr. Byrd. A park was built in honor of Mr. James Byrd. The park bears his name and rightfully so. I think it is good to look back at history, to gain perspective for the present, to plan for the future, and hopefully not make the same mistake again.

I feel like the town of Jasper has made a considerable recovery from the nightmare that occurred about a decade ago.

Many of the residents in Jasper want the world to also know the "up" side of Jasper. For example, Jasper is now the home of American Idol and national singing star, Michael Sarver. There is a large banner in Jasper, where highway 190 intersects highway 96. The banner reads Michael Sarver, American Idol.

Jasper is also the home of international track and field star Bryan Bronson. It is the home of professional football star Robert "Big Red" Bryant.

Jasper is the home of the All-American linebacker of the University of Missouri., Sean Weatherspoon. It is also the home of one of the all time greatest track coaches who ever lived, the late Lloyd Weatherspoon. He won 15 district championships and 3 state champions in Texas High School track and field 4A division.

It is the home of the first black principal in the history of Jasper High School, Mr. Victor Williams. It is home to the first white principal at Rowe Intermediate School, Mrs. Stacey Woolems. It is the home of Few and Parnell Elementary schools. They both are "exemplary" schools for 2009. This is the highest rating a school in Texas can receive for academic excellence.

Jasper is home to the 2007 3A High School champions in baseball, the Jasper Bulldog baseball team. It is home to one of the top all girl soccer teams in the nation, the Twisters. Jasper is home to an all girl summer league track team that won numerous district, regional, state and national awards from 1996 – 2000. The track team was called the Tigerbelles. It is also home to the state championship track team of 1991, the Jasper Varsity High School Girls Track Team, who won the state title in division 4A.

Jasper is home to the Belle-Jim Hotel, a 100 year old national monument, which still has one of the best restaurants in town.

It is home to a brilliant first year teacher named Joshelyn Strother, who is following in the footsteps of her mother, Martha Adams, as a dedicated teacher.

Jasper is home to the Horns, Hadnots, Lands, Haffords, Chimneys, Clevelands, Kenebrews, Sells, Diggles, and other prominent black families who have been here for decades. It is also home to the Alvises, Ratcliffs, Ebarbs, Barabasses, Kipps, Primroses, Bebees, Frizzells, and other prominent white families who have been here for decades.

Jasper is a place where if you say "Good Morning" to anyone black or white that 9 times out of 10 that person will respond with a good morning back to you. It is a place where school age children from elementary school, to junior high to high school for the most part still say yes ma'am and no ma'am, yes sir and no sir when addressing or answering adults.

Recently Mr. Bob Love, who was a former 3 time NBA all star with the Chicago Bulls gave a motivational speech to some student athletes at Jasper High. He normally charges $15,000 per hr. for his speeches around the country. He gave Jasper high this session for free. The main theme of his speech was never let go of your dreams.

The common denominator in all of this is that all of us hope for and some of us pray for a better day. We hope for a better life for our children. It is no different in Jasper.

One of the main residents of Jasper is "hope". Hope still resides in Jasper. Yes, in Jasper, hope is alive and well and gaining momentum.

MEMORY PAGES

Perhaps you live in a town or area where Martha lived. You may want to ask someone who knew her to write down briefly their memories of her. An example is given that was written by one of Martha's best friends in Jasper.

If you don't live in the same area as Martha did, then perhaps you know of someone in your family who had a similar experience. You may do a brief write up on them or ask someone who knew them to do it or ask the person to do it. People who had a similar experience to Martha are out there. There may be one living in your neighborhood.

My Memories of Martha (Mackie) Adams

Martha was a very loving and caring person. She had a beautiful smile that would light up the whole world! She loved her family and community. Martha had many friends in her lifetime. I am proud to say that I was one of her friends. I addressed her by her nickname "Mackie".

We became neighbors in August of 1993 and remained neighbors until her death April of 2005. When I didn't have a car, Martha would take me places I needed to go. Sometime she would allow me to drive her car. My daughter Courtney and Martha's daughter Joshelyn are good friends. We would talk about our children and life in general. She was always encouraging me. I also remember Martha's mother, who was a great beautician and hair dresser.

In Martha's professional life, she was a dedicated and wonderful teacher. She also had beautiful handwriting. Martha inspired me to become a teacher. Her daughter Joshelyn went on to college to become a teacher. She teaches 6th Grade Language Arts. I really miss talking to Mackie. She was a once in a lifetime friend.

Hazel Patricia Larkin

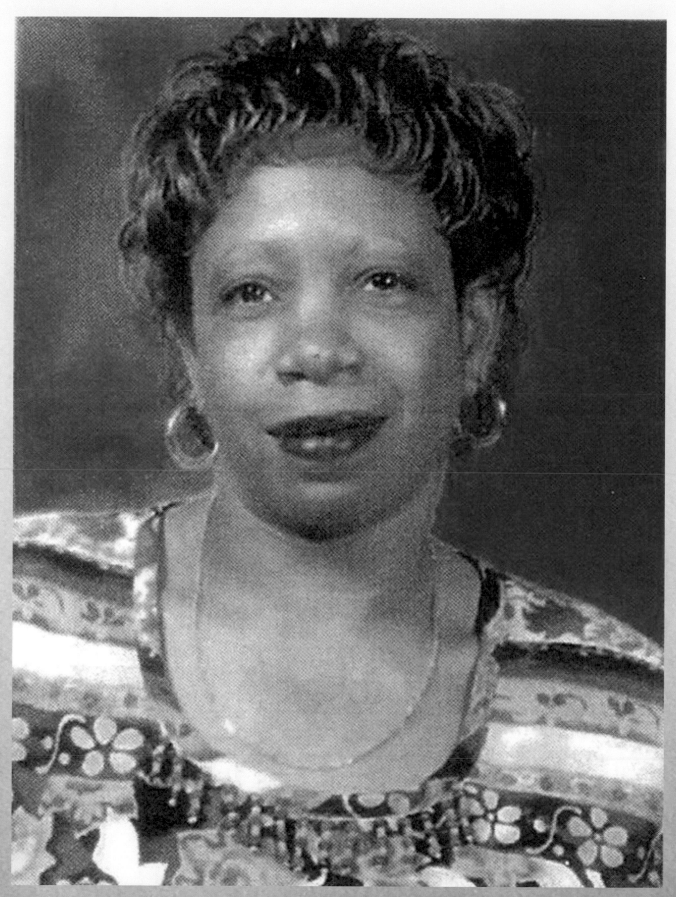

Martha Maxine "Mackie" Adams

Memory Writing Page

Memory Pictorial Page

Printed in the United States
By Bookmasters